LET THE GAMES BEGIN!

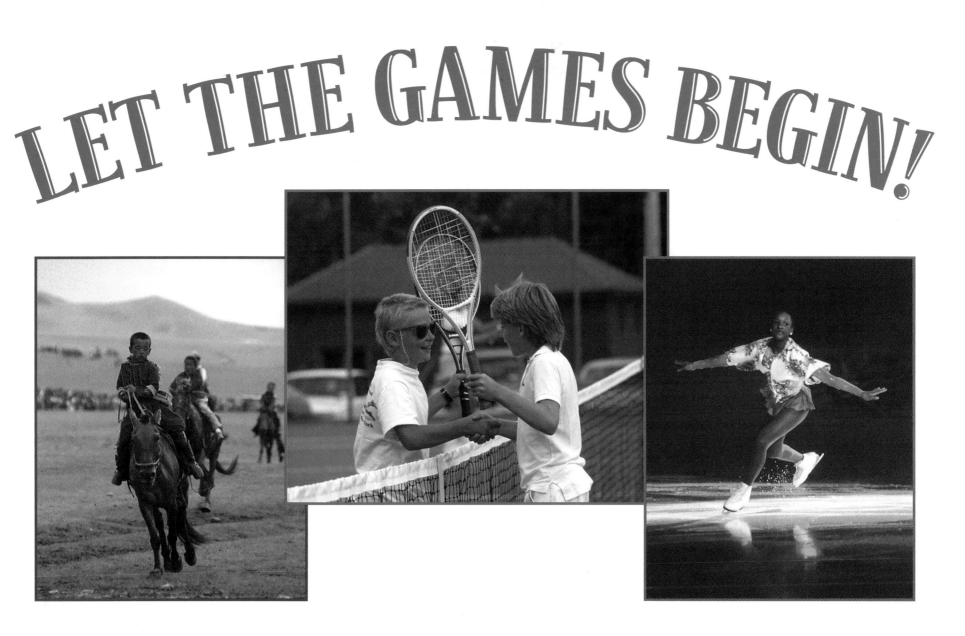

Maya Ajmera   with a foreword by Bill Bradley   **Michael J. Regan**

SHAKTI for Children

Charlesbridge

The game that is called soccer in the United States is called football in other countries. Captions for pictures of this sport include both names, with the American name listed first. The game Americans call football is played almost exclusively in the United States.

Foreword

On any given day, millions of kids around the globe are playing sports. Why? First and foremost, to have fun. Sports are about having a good time. They are also about life. Sports help young people develop and teach them important lessons:

- To finish a game, especially when you are tired, you must persevere.

- To overcome an injury and get back into the game, you need courage.

- To believe you can win a close game, you need to have confidence in yourself and your teammates.

- To be part of a successful team, you must understand and practice teamwork.

Sports were an important part of my childhood. At an early age, I began playing baseball, basketball, and whatever else was in season. My love of sports led me to a successful basketball career, an Olympic gold medal, and many valuable friendships. The lessons I learned from sports have served me well throughout my life, both on and off the court.

Let the Games Begin! captures the joy of sports and shares so many reasons for getting involved. No matter where you live or what your level of skill or experience, sports can play an important role in your life. I hope this book will be an inspiration to you.

Bill Bradley
U.S. Senate, 1979–1997
New York Knicks, 1967–1977

Basketball in Turkey and Ecuador. Soccer in Guatemala

Basketball   Ecuador

Wherever you live, you can enjoy sports. You might like making a basket, scoring a goal, running a race, or hitting a bull's-eye. There are lots of choices.

Soccer/Football   Guatemala

Swimming in Benin and Mexico. Tennis in Ukraine

and Zimbabwe. Cricket in India and the United Kingdom.

Kids all over the world like sports for the fun, for the friendship, and for the challenge. No matter what sport you play, something exciting and wonderful can happen at any moment.

Track and Field   United States

Archery   Bhutan

and the United States. Skiing in China and Finland.

> *"I think that everyone should have one or more goals. In this way, they can improve each day."*
> —Diego, Costa Rica

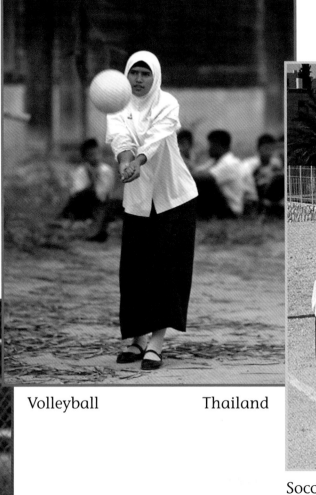

Volleyball   Thailand

Soccer/Football

Baseball   United States

Sports give you a chance to dream. Imagine being as great as your favorite athlete. You can see yourself hitting a home run, skating the perfect program, or making the winning shot. When you dream, anything seems possible!

Israel

Ice-Skating   Russia

Golf   United States

Reach for your dreams by setting goals. Choosing the right goals—ones that aren't too easy or too hard—helps you get to the next level. You might be into sports just for fun, or you might hope to win a championship. Either way, you learn and improve each time you play.

Most kids get started in sports by playing with their friends. After school, it's fun to go swimming or shoot hoops. There are lots of ways to get involved. Try a team sport like softball, cricket, ice hockey, or volleyball. Or choose a sport you can do on your own, like golf, skiing, horseback riding, or gymnastics.

Golf

Kung Fu   China

Swimming   Mexico

Play different sports to learn which ones you like most. Your friends, family, and coaches can give you advice. But nobody can tell you what it really feels like to swing a golf club or serve a badminton birdie. To learn a sport, you have to jump into the action.

India

Baseball

United States

Skiing

Finland

> *"My body feels energized and in control when I play."*
> —Greg, United States

Running, jumping, kicking, and flying through the air—in sports you use your body in lots of different ways. You leap, bend, and turn during a gymnastics routine. You wind up to pitch a baseball, crouch as you approach a ski jump, and charge down the field after a soccer ball. Just by playing, you build strength, speed, balance, and coordination.

Gymnastics

Ice-Skating

In-Line Skating   Australia

United States

Democratic Republic
of Congo

Gymnastics   China

Soccer/Football   Bolivia

As your body grows and changes, so do your abilities. You become stronger and more confident as you test yourself in new ways. Movements that once felt difficult, like passing a soccer ball or doing a backbend, start to feel natural. You are becoming an athlete!

> *"Practice is the only way to improve and get better at your sport."*
> —Anders, Norway

Cricket   India

Gymnastics

Swimming   Benin

Mastering a sport takes hard work and, most of all, practice. Even the greatest athletes practice for hours every day. Tennis players hit forehands and backhands, over and over again. Gymnasts repeat the same routine for hours. From practice you gain concentration and self-discipline, which are needed for success in any sport.

United States

Swimming   Mexico

Tennis   Portugal

When you play organized sports, you have coaches to guide and support you. They teach you the basic skills, like how to swim freestyle or how to swing a cricket bat. The best coaches help you learn at your own pace and in your own way. During practice and competition, coaches are there for you when you need them most.

You're likely to hit obstacles as you play sports. Maybe you can't master a new skill, or a challenge looks too hard. Competing in a difficult match or riding in a championship race can make you nervous or wear you out. These feelings are natural. Don't give up!

Tennis   United States

Cricket

Football   United States

Biking   Japan

India

Soccer/Football   United Kingdom

Practice, advice, and encouragement
help you overcome obstacles. One day,
you will face and beat your fear of
jumping off the high board or handle
the pressure of taking a last-second shot.
By challenging you, sports help you
discover just how strong you really are.

> *"Playing by the rules means not to cheat, to respect other people, and to be honest."*
> —Staci, Russia

Ice Hockey

Basketball   United States

Soccer/Football   United States

Rules! Who needs them? You do, to play a sport. Rules tell you how to play a game, and what's fair or unfair. In soccer and basketball, the rules tell you how to pass and score points, and what happens when the rules are broken. Rules even tell you what kind of ball to use—after all, the whole game would change if you tried to kick a baseball or dribble a tennis ball.

Rules don't work if people ignore them, so most competitive sports have referees, umpires, or judges. These officials take action if someone breaks a rule. In volleyball, if you hit the net while spiking the ball, your team doesn't score the point. In the one-hundred-meter dash, you get disqualified if you leave your own lane. Games are more fun if everyone plays by the rules!

United States
vs. Canada

Volleyball   Dominican Republic

Track and Field   Sierra Leone

Golf   United States

Soccer/Football

Karate   Indonesia

The way you act helps make a game both fun and fair. In golf, you keep track of your own score. You even call penalties on yourself for breaking a rule, such as accidentally touching the ball before a shot. Being honest is part of being a good sport.

Being a good sport also means that you respect other players at all times. A courageous athlete plays hard but never tries to injure another player, even in contact sports like karate, football, and rugby. Good sportsmanship is global— around the world it's the sign of a champion.

Ghana

Ice Hockey

Canada

Tennis

United States

> *"Working together as a team means covering, helping, and basically being there for each other."*
> —Chenserai, Swaziland

To play a team sport you need to cooperate. You might want to drive to the hoop in basketball. Instead, you pass the ball to a player who has an open shot. Helping your team score points is always more important than how good you look.

Badminton

Basketball   Philippines

Track and Field   Swaziland

United States

Soccer/Football United States

Ice Hockey Canada

In team sports, players learn to communicate with each other in new ways. With a look or a nod of your head, you can tell a teammate where to pass the hockey puck. You make a sudden move, and before your opponents can react, you are breaking open toward the goal. Good teams create a magic that makes them better than their individual players.

> *"In a small way I am a leader because younger swimmers look up to me."*
> —Em-Em, Philippines

Everybody can be a leader! Leaders emerge through their skill, attitude, or commitment to the team. The captain of the equestrian team isn't always the best horseback rider. He or she is someone who knows how to motivate the team and how to help teammates through tough situations.

Horseback Riding   United States

Soccer/Football   Brazil

Softball

Skiing   China

Soccer/Football   Argentina

United States

Different players can be leaders at different times. A goalie can shout guidance across the field or keep the other team from scoring. Players on the sidelines can cheer encouragement as their team heads up and down the field. In sports, there are lots of ways to make a difference.

> *"Competition is good because it creates a challenge. Without challenges, life would be boring."*
> —Hayley, South Africa

Competition is a big part of sports. To get ready for an event, you and your teammates work harder. Once the contest starts, making a perfect dive, scoring a goal, or winning a race can seem like the most important thing in the world.

Horseback Riding

Gymnastics   Romania

Soccer/Football   Pakistan

During the heat of competition, strong opponents push each other to do better. In a close contest, no one can take it easy. Feeling another runner right on your heels or seeing one just ahead helps you find an extra burst of speed. Successful athletes learn to do their best under pressure.

Mongolia

Judo

United States

Track and Field

United Kingdom

> *"Everyone likes to win, and you can if you work hard."*
> —Sophia, Portugal

Everybody wants to win. When you do, you feel a rush of excitement. Winning the fifty-meter freestyle makes all your hours of swimming laps worthwhile. When you come from behind or win when you weren't expected to, the victory tastes especially sweet.

Basketball

Track and Field   Swaziland

Track and Field   United States

No one likes to lose. If your team fails to block the winning shot in the championship game, you feel upset and maybe even angry. But doing your best is what matters most. Understanding what went wrong will help you the next time. And win or lose, a true champion accepts the outcome gracefully.

Colombia

Volleyball   Eritrea

Basketball   United States

> *"Friendship is important for the team, because if you aren't friends the team won't play well."*
> —Nicols, Bulgaria

Playing sports is a great way to meet new friends. When you support each other on and off the field, you grow to trust and count on each other.

Fans

Basketball   Kenya

Soccer/Football   United Kingdom

You become better friends by sharing the laughter and celebration of winning and the tears and disappointment of losing. Some of the friendships that develop through sports last a lifetime.

Japan

Wrestling   United States

Fans   Bolivia

Many families and friends go to sporting events together. They support and cheer for their favorite players and teams. Fans shout and clap, wave signs and flags, wear team colors, and even paint their faces. Athletes and spectators look forward not just to the games, but to the time spent with friends and family. Sports bring people together all over the world.

"I like learning more and more about the sport I love."
—Polina, Ukraine

You have a lot in common with young athletes around the world. Everywhere kids play sports they practice, learn new skills, and build strong, healthy bodies. They feel joy, excitement, pressure, and the thrill of competition. And no matter where they live or what sport they play, they feel happy when they win and sad when they lose.

Cricket

Tennis   Ukraine

Ski Jumpers   United States

India

Soccer/Football   Dominican Republic

Soccer/Football   Ecuador

Some kids like sports for the exercise or the excitement. Some love the challenge of trying to be the best. And some just have fun spending time with their friends. There are lots of reasons to play sports. Pick the one that's right for you, and let the games begin!

This book is dedicated to my brother, Ravi,
a swimmer and an all-around athlete.
—M.A.

Special blessings for my grandmother, Gertrude Regan, who encouraged
me to have fun, speak the truth, and be my own person.
—M.R.

Financial support for this project has been provided by the Tiger Woods Foundation, the Women's Sports Foundation, and the W.K. Kellogg Foundation.

Our heartfelt thanks to Kelly Swanson Turner, editor of SHAKTI for Children/ Charlesbridge books, for providing insightful comments and wisdom throughout the project. Additional thanks to Charlesbridge senior editor Harold Underdown and to Charlesbridge designer Diane Earley for her superb book design.

As always, deepest thanks to the photographers. We have worked with many of them on previous projects, and we also welcome many new contributors with *Let the Games Begin!* Without their photographs, there would simply be no book.

We are grateful to Bill Bradley for his inspiring foreword and to Ed Turlington and Eric Hauser of Mr. Bradley's office. Thank you to Anita DeFrantz of the Amateur Athletic Foundation and Coach Mike Krzyzewski of the Duke University men's basketball team for their words of wisdom and praise.

The creative thinking and guidance for *Let the Games Begin!* came from many individuals, including: Byron Shewman, Starlings Volleyball Clubs; Brad Smith, *Sports Illustrated for Kids*; Keith Cruickshank and Wayne Wilson, Amateur Athletic Foundation; Michelle Bemis, Tiger Woods Foundation; Quin Snyder, the University of Missouri at Columbia's men's basketball team; and George Adams, Ravi Ajmera, Nancie Battaglia, Katie Bell, Fritz Mayer, Sanjay Mullick, Olateju Omolodun, Maia Chang Rosen, Bob Service, Susan Slotter, and Sarah Strunk. Special thanks to our colleagues and the board of directors of the Global Fund for Children.

Let the Games Begin! is a project of SHAKTI for Children, which is dedicated to teaching children to value diversity and to grow into productive, caring citizens of the world. SHAKTI for Children is a program of the Global Fund for Children (www.globalfundforchildren.org).

Published by Charlesbridge Publishing
85 Main Street, Watertown, MA 02472
(617) 926-0329
www.charlesbridge.com

Developed by SHAKTI for Children
The Global Fund for Children
1612 K Street N.W., Suite 706, Washington, DC 20006
(202) 331-9003
www.shakti.org

Details about the donation of royalties can be obtained by writing to Charlesbridge Publishing and SHAKTI for Children.

Library of Congress Cataloging-in-Publication Data
Ajmera, Maya.
Let the games begin!/Maya Ajmera and Michael Regan; developed by Shakti for Children; with a foreword by Bill Bradley.
    p.   cm.
Summary: Text and photographs of children from around the world focus on various aspects of sports, including physical benefits, the importance of practice, overcoming obstacles, teamwork, and more.
    ISBN 0-88106-067-4 (reinforced for library use)
    ISBN 0-88106-068-2 (softcover)
1. Sports for children—Juvenile literature. 2. Sportsmanship—Juvenile literature. [1. Sports.] I. Regan, Michael (Michael J.), 1962- . II. Shakti for Children (Organization). III. Title.
GV709.2.A43   2000
796—dc21   99-24032

Printed in South Korea
(hc) 10 9 8 7 6 5 4 3 2 1
(sc) 10 9 8 7 6 5 4 3 2 1

The display type and text type were set in Jimbo and Stone Informal.
Scans were produced by ARTSLIDES, Somerville, Massachusetts.
Color separations were made by Sung In Printing, Inc., South Korea.
Printed and bound by Sung In Printing, Inc., South Korea
Production supervision by Brian G. Walker
Designed by Diane M. Earley

Other SHAKTI for Children/Charlesbridge Books

Children from Australia to Zimbabwe: A Photographic Journey around the World by Maya Ajmera and Anna Rhesa Versola

Extraordinary Girls by Maya Ajmera, Olateju Omolodun, and Sarah Strunk

To Be a Kid by Maya Ajmera and John Ivanko

Xanadu, the Imaginary Place: A Showcase of Writings and Artwork by North Carolina's Children edited by Maya Ajmera and Olateju Omolodun

Photographs (left to right unless otherwise noted): *Cover* (clockwise from upper left): © Monkmeyer/Bopp, © Steve Lange, © Jon Warren, © Nancie Battaglia, © Richard T. Nowitz; *Title Page:* © Nik Wheeler, © Nancie Battaglia, © Nancie Battaglia; *Pages 2-3* (clockwise from bottom of page 2): © Nik Wheeler, © Dinodia/V.H. Mishra, © Cynthia Lum, © Steve Lange, © Nik Wheeler, © Steve Lange, © Nik Wheeler; *Pages 4-5:* © Melissa Farlow, © Jim Adriance, © Amateur Athletic Foundation, © Jon Warren; *Pages 6-7:* © Monkmeyer/Kopstein, © Nik Wheeler, © Monkmeyer/Wolf, © Monkmeyer/Siteman, © Bill Bachmann/Network Aspen; *Pages 8-9:* © Stephanie Maze, © Nik Wheeler, © Dinodia/N.M. Jain, © Karim Shamsi-Basha, © Nik Wheeler; *Pages 10-11:* © Nancie Battaglia, © John D. Ivanko, © Jon Warren, © Steve Lange, © Jon Warren; *Pages 12-13:* © Mary Altier, © Julia Dean, © Dave Black, © Stephanie Maze, © Nik Wheeler; *Pages 14-15:* © Steve Lange, © Nik Wheeler, © Catherine Karnow, © Richard T. Nowitz, © Dominic Dibbs; *Pages 16-17:* © Richard T. Nowitz, © Nik Wheeler, © Nancie Battaglia, © Monkmeyer/Bopp, © Lauralea Gulpin; *Pages 18-19:* © Nik Wheeler, © David Lissy/Network Aspen, © Mary Altier, © Jan Reynolds, © Nancie Battaglia; *Pages 20-21:* © Debbie Simerlink, © Elaine Little, © Amateur Athletic Foundation, © Nik Wheeler, © Nik Wheeler; *Pages 22-23:* © Eastcott/Momatiuk/Woodfin Camp, © Michelle A. Zweede, © Stephanie Maze, © Jan Reynolds, © Monkmeyer/Sanguinetti; *Pages 24-25:* © Nik Wheeler, © Steve Lange, © Nik Wheeler, © Nile Sprague, © Nancie Battaglia; *Pages 26-27:* © Nancie Battaglia, © Debbie Simerlink, © Jon Warren, © Wendy Miller, © Karim Shamsi-Basha; *Pages 28-29:* © Rena Pugh, © Nile Sprague, © Nancie Battaglia, © Karim Shamsi-Basha, © Jon Warren; *Pages 30-31:* © Bob Olness, © Nancie Battaglia, © Dinodia/Mishra, © Monkmeyer/Bopp, © John D. Ivanko; *Back Cover:* © Jon Warren, © Monkmeyer/Siteman.